IVERPOOL & THE MERSEY

~ *a nostalgic pictorial journey* ~

Peter W. Woolley

SIGMA

Published by Sigma Leisure – an imprint of Sigma Press, 1 South Oak Lane, Wilmslow, Cheshire SK9 6AR, England.

British Library Cataloguing in Publication Data
A CIP record for this book is available from the British Library.

ISBN: 1-85058-670-5

Cover photographs: left, members of the Merseyside Police Mounted Department wearing ceremonial uniforms, with the Royal Liver Buildings as a backdrop; top, *MV Britannic* of the White Star line, c. 1935; bottom, 1911 map of the River Mersey, issued by Cadburys and used as a reward card in schools for good work or attendance.

Typesetting and Design by: Sigma Press, Wilmslow, Cheshire.

Printed by: MFP Design and Print

Preface

This book takes the reader on a guided tour of the city of Liverpool showing some of the fine buildings, theatres, cinemas, shops, churches and places of entertainment. In some cases, along with the original view, a modern photograph has been taken to show some of the changes that have taken place in the city centre. After the city centre tour, we head out through the suburbs, past Liverpool Airport, and on to the Runcom transporter bridge, from where we continue along the River Mersey showing the varied ships that sailed the Mersey at the time of Liverpool's greatest prosperity, and up to the present day. I have tried to include as many previously unpublished photographs as possible, including a number I have taken myself.

Liverpool has an illustrious past and a fascinating maritime heritage. In 1207, King John granted a Charter to Liverpool – then a small fishing village on the east bank of the estuary of the River Mersey. During the next 500 years, the village grew to a sizeable town and fishing port, with many of its population going to sea to earn their living to support their families.

At the beginning of the eighteenth century, far-sighted merchants saw the possibilities of using Liverpool as a trading port. Geographically, it provided an ideal situation due to its proximity to the industrial Midlands. The first wet dock was constructed in 1715. However, its initial development was hampered by the shifting sand banks which obstructed the mouth of the Mersey Estuary, leaving only 11ft of water at low tide. Large vessels either had to wait for a suitable tide, or partially unload close to the Wirral peninsula. Dredging began at the end of the nineteenth century, which provided a temporary solution to the problem. Eventually a remedy was found by dumping limestone along the sandbanks, which prevented further erosion. By 1960, there were 20 miles of submerged limestone embankment, which maintained a depth of 25ft at low water in the Crosby channel.

The Industrial Revolution and the growth of international trade during the nineteenth century resulted in the dramatic growth of the port of Liverpool. Several new docks were built to accommodate the increasing number of ships visiting the port, and many enterprising shipping companies established their bases in Liverpool. In addition, it became a major transatlantic port for the shipment of mail, as well as the embarkation point for the increasing number of emigrants leaving for America, who were attracted by the promises of wealth and new opportunities.

Along with the docks, the city centre expanded rapidly, with many fine houses being built for the wealthy shipowners and merchants, along with business premises near to the docks. To accommodate the dock workers and their families, poor quality back-to-back housing and the infamous court-type dwellings (small enclosed streets, having a yard surrounded by slum houses) were erected in close proximity to the docks. Due to the general level of poverty, crime was rife both in the city and the docks. Immigrants especially, who often could speak little or no English, were an easy target for the thieves, robbers and prostitutes of the city. There are still a number of buildings in Liverpool that remind us of those dark days, though most have been demolished. Better housing, hospitals and schools helped the city to prosper. Hand in hand with these developments came improvements in drinking water and sewerage treatments.

The 'Mersey Docks and Harbour Board' was formed in 1857, which also included the Birkenhead Docks. By the beginning of the twentieth century, Liverpool had become the nation's second port (after London) and boasted one of the most impressive waterfronts in Britain: six-and-a-half miles of docks (Gladstone to Dingle oil jetty) with Garston Docks three miles further upstream. On the southern side of the Mersey Estuary, the dock system included: the Birkenhead Docks; Cammell Laird & Co; the Tranmere oil terminal; Port Sunlight; Bromborough Docks; and the Eastern Locks, which form part of the entrance to the Manchester Ship Canal. In total, sixty-five wet docks, and twenty-two dry, or graving docks. The lineal quayage measured over thirty-six miles, with a surface of water covering six hundred acres.

In the late 1960s and the early 1970s, the introduction of containerisation and the opening of Seaforth Docks, heralded the demise of traditional cargo handling methods. This resulted in the gradual closure and subsequent decay of many docks and quayside buildings. During the 1980s, a dramatic reversal occurred with many of the old docks being renovated and reclaimed to provide recreation, tourist facilities, and new business properties – the Albert Dock being one of the country's leading tourist attractions. On the commercial front, the Northern Docks and the Seaforth Container Terminal have reported handling record tonnage.

I am pleased to acknowledge the assistance given to me by many people, including: Albert Howarth; Ian Boumphrey; Wirral Postcards; Mrs. Edna Pye; Mrs. Linda Brown; Merseyside Police; Runcorn Library; Bootle Historical Society; Raymond Patrick (Bootle Times).

Peter W. Woolley

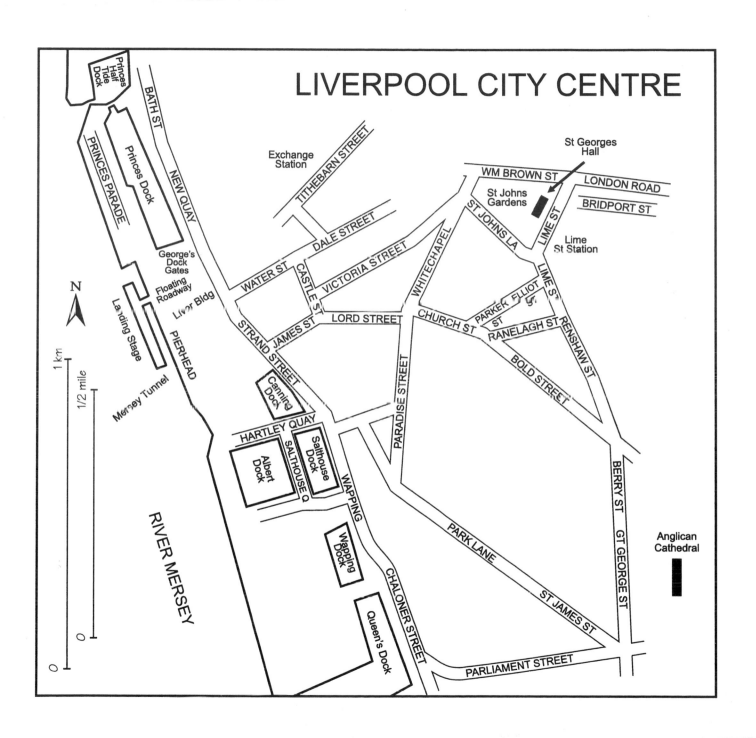

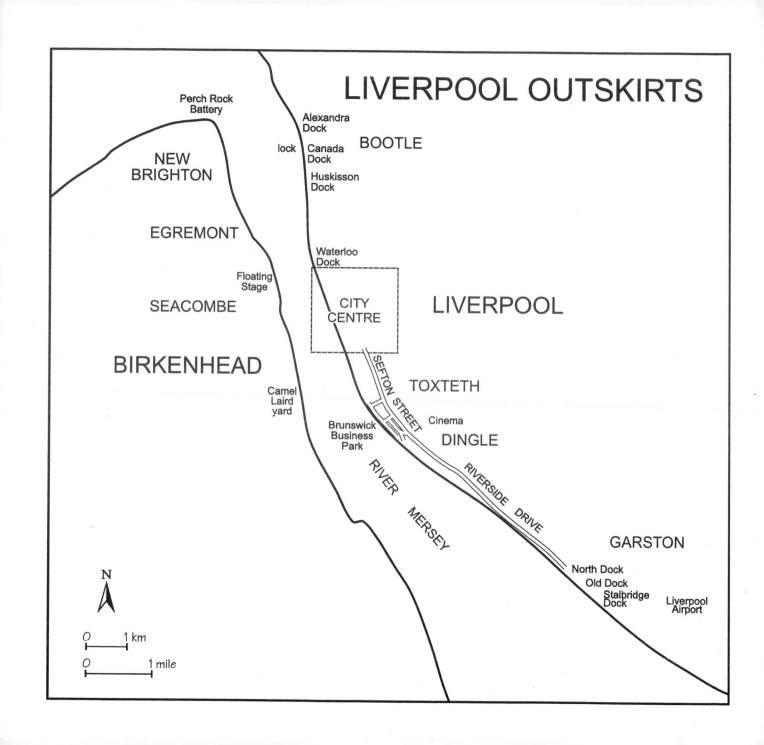

The City and Suburbs

Liverpool Coat of Arms. In the centre of the shield is a cormorant, commonly referred to as a "Liver" – hence 'Liver bird'. It is holding a branch of seaweed known as a "laver". Above the shield, the crest is comprised of a cormorant with its wings elevated also holding a branch of seaweed and standing on a wreath. The origin of the Liver bird is obscure but its use on the shield is probably derived from the common seal of the town, the original being lost during the siege of 1644. The latter is thought to have included the eagle of St John, which is believed to have been modified to look like a cormorant; the Fleur-de-Lys on the seal was altered to seaweed (or laver). The supporters were granted on 23rd March 1797. On the left hand side of the shield is Neptune wearing a gold crown, a green mantle wreathed with laver and holding a trident and banner with the arms of Liverpool. On the right-hand side of the shield Triton is shown blowing a shell and holding a banner depicting a ship under sail. The Latin motto translated is "God has given this leisure to us".

Note: throughout this book, "p.u." indicates "postally used" – i.e. a postcard that has been through the postal system of the time

Liverpool in the 17th century. An artist's impression of Liverpool viewed from Birkenhead and published on a postcard c.1912. St Nicholas's church is visible on the left; this is known as the sailors' church. It is the oldest Anglican church in Liverpool and was originally built in the mid-14th century. To the right, the castle is now the site of the Queen Victoria monument in Derby Square.

George's Dock. Another artist's impression of Liverpool's waterfront, showing George's Dock, constructed in 1771 at a cost of £21,000. St Nicholas's church is to be seen to the left. The Goree piazzas are in the centre, with St George's church to the right in the background. This postcard was published by Clydesdale & Jennings Ltd, in their *Ancient Liverpool* series.

The Mariners' Church. The Mariners' Church was situated in George's dock. The church was originally a government-owned guard-ship named the *Tees*, deployed to protect the Atlantic island of St Helena. The ship was converted to a church in 1826 with space for 1,000 worshippers at a time. The Mariners' Church sank on 27th June 1872, due to lack of maintenance and natural decay of its framework. This postcard was also one of the *Ancient Liverpool* series.

Multiview of Liverpool. c.1905. Twelve small views of Liverpool on one postcard. Top, left to right: The Town Hall; William Brown Street; Lime Street; Exchange Flags. Centre: Sefton Park; Technical School; a Pilot Boat; Gladstone's Birthplace. Bottom Row: A Mersey Ferry; Landing Stage; the arrival of Lucania; the Palm House, Sefton Park.

LIVERPOOL *from the Air.*

Liverpool from the air. c.1925. This superb aerial view shows the rooftops of the County Sessions House, the Walker Art Gallery and, on the right, part of St George's Hall. Also visible are the Wellington Monument, Steble Fountain, Commutation Row, London Road, the Legs of Man public house, the Empire Theatre, Frazer Street, and the Shakespeare Theatre. In London Road, behind the Empire, was the stadium used for boxing. This was demolished and the Paramount Cinema (later, the Odeon) was built on the site.

London Road. c.1956. Looking up London Road from Commutation Row we see some of the shops and businesses that no longer exist. Most prominent is "Jeromes" the photographers – there is hardly a local family that has not had their photographs taken by them. Other shops include Hepworths, tailors and gents' outfitters; Halfords, the cycle dealers; Weaver to Wearer and Jackson's, both tailors. On the right is the Odeon cinema, showing a Gary Cooper film. To complete the picture a 6A tram is heading up towards Monument Place.

Jeromes. c.1935. Advertised as the originators of the postcard print from a small camera. Some of their photographs were printed postcard size for ease of sending through the post. The name "Jerome" stood for quality and satisfaction. They had many shops up and down the country, but their main works were in Bovey Place, Holloway, London. Illustrated is one of their photograph and negative folders, which was beige in colour with printing in black, white and orange.

Monument Place. c.1930. Situated at the junction of London Road and Pembroke Place. Businesses included Alexandra Furnishings and of course T.J. Hughes, the department store. The equestrian statue on Monument Place is of George III. It was designed by Robert Westmacott, RA. Monument Place also had below-ground Ladies' and Gents' toilets.

Bridport Street. c.1912. This lovely postcard is of J.C. Clarke's grocery shop, at the corner of Bridport Street and Seymour Street, off London Road. It is of historical interest as the photograph was taken shortly after the *Titanic* disaster was made known. One of the advertisement boards shows a *Liverpool Echo* poster "TITANIC DISASTER, LIST OF SURVIVORS". It is thought to have been the first shop in Liverpool to report the disaster. Also visible are the *Daily Sketch* board, TITANIC'S FAREWELL and the *Daily News*, LIST OF SURVIVORS. The shop remained in the family until the late 1960s. It remained derelict for many years until demolished in the 1970s.

Joseph Wigglesworth. c.1909. One of Liverpool's most well-known characters. He lost both of his legs at the age of 13 when he fell off a cliff. For thirty-odd years he could be seen in Pudsey Street, off London Road. He sat on his cart summer and winter, along with his faithful dog, soliciting for alms from passers-by, including theatre and cinema patrons. He lived close by in a first-floor flat in Bridport Street. He died in April 1911, aged 94, of bronchitis.

The Steble Fountain. c.1900. This magnificent fountain was a gift presented to Liverpool on 3rd May 1879 by Lt. Col. Steble, a former Lord Mayor of the city. On the left is St George's Hall. The clock tower of the Municipal building is in the centre with, in front, the Old Haymarket, which later made way for the entrance to the Mersey Tunnel. In the Old Haymarket were: Doyles, the tailors; Husbands, gents' hats; Cambell and Mabb, ironmongers and tools; Ma Noblet's, confectioners and The Cocoa Rooms; Liptons, tea merchants. The raised road leading to the museum was later demolished to the level of William Brown Street and steps put in its place.

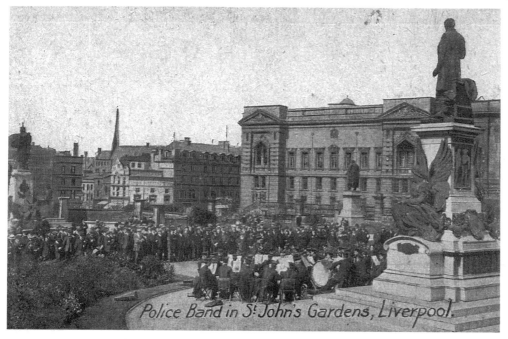

Police Band in S.* John's Gardens, Liverpool.

St John's Gardens. c.1920. A pleasant afternoon is being enjoyed by the audience listening to the Liverpool City police band. Citizens of Liverpool and later Merseyside have enjoyed the police band for many years. Not only do they play at official functions, they also visit parks and gardens, schools and sheltered accommodation. Opposite the gardens and originally the site of St John's church, is the Liverpool City Museum, which extends to the junction of Byrom Street.

View from Victoria Street. p.u.1912. This picture of a busy junction was taken from Victoria Street, looking towards William Brown Street and St John's Gardens. On the left is a Liverpool city police officer wearing his white summer helmet. It was made of compressed straw for lightness. To his right is a 'Coopers' delivery van. To the right of St John's Gardens are the premises of J. Hughes, the Temperance Hotel and the Army recruiting office.

**William Brown Street.
p.u.1913**. Two young ladies
in their finery seem to be in
a great hurry towards Dale
Street, while two street
urchins lean against a
bollard and a tram climbs
towards Lime Street. On the
left are the museum, the
Walker Art Gallery and the
Picton Library. The
Wellington Monument is
prominent at the top. It was
erected to commemorate the
victories of the Duke of
Wellington. It is 115 feet
high and the 14-foot-high
statue of Wellington on the
top was cast from cannons
and trophies captured at the
Battle of Waterloo.

OPENING OF THE MERSEY TUNNEL. 1934. L.V. 23.

The Mersey Tunnel. c.1934.
When completed, the Mersey
Tunnel was described as one
of the seven wonders of the
world. Work commenced in
1925 and twin pilot tunnels
were driven from both banks
of the Mersey at Birkenhead
and Liverpool. These were
excavated to form the
44-foot-wide tunnels. The
tunnel was opened by King
George V, accompanied by
Queen Mary. After the
ceremony the King was
presented with a model of
the tunnel entrance. Local
school children received a
medal to commemorate the
occasion.

St John's Lane. c.1910. This unusual photograph was taken in the depths of winter by an unknown photographer who, after taking this shot, must have been frozen stiff. In the background are St John's gardens with the statue of Major Lester in front of the rear of St George's Hall.

St George's Plateau. c.1931. Fronting St George's Hall, facing the Empire theatre and the London and North Western Railway hotel, is this majestic plateau. On plinths, there are four lions 'passant'. Looking towards the hall there are the statues: Albert, The Prince Consort; The Earl of Beaconsfield; on her horse is Queen Victoria; just out of the picture is Major General William Earl C.B., C.S.I. He was killed in the Sudan in 1885.

The Liverpool Cenotaph. c.1925. This moving scene in Lime Street, on St George's Hall plateau, was taken during a Remembrance Service. A good vantage point was on the roof of the Empire Theatre, which can be seen with its flag at half-mast. To its left is the Legs of Man public house and on the other side of London Road is Burton's the Tailors.

Liverpool Cenotaph

Lime Street and Empire Theatre, Liverpool

The Empire Theatre. c.1920. The theatre was originally opened in 1866 as the New Prince of Wales and Italian Opera House, changing its name to the Royal Alexander Theatre and Opera House in 1867. It was renamed the Empire in 1895 and was demolished in 1923. It reopened in 1925 and is one of the largest theatres in the country. It can accommodate in excess of 3,000 patrons. It is at present undergoing refurbishment and extensions, said to incorporate the Legs of Man public house next door.

Lime Street. c.1900. This is one of my favourite photographs, taken by William Thomas Wright of Bootle. It shows Lime Street at its busiest. A horse and cart stands motionless on the cobbles alongside a Hansom cab waiting for a fare. Behind it is a water cart heading for St John's Lane. Gossiping on the pavement is a group of 'Mary Ellens' - Liverpool's flower sellers - with their baskets and their unusual headgear, to used to carry baskets on top of one another, sometimes up to six at a time.

Lime Street. c.1905. A view of Lime Street from St George's plateau, showing lots of activity. Professor Codman's Punch and Judy show can be seen (see also next page) - its location was designated by the Post Office as No. 1, Lime Street, Liverpool. The show had a large audience of all ages – some delivery boys with their handcarts have stopped to watch. Buildings, right to left are: the Reynolds Animated Picture House; Washington Hotel; Imperial Hotel and St George Hotel. On the left is Menzie & Co, jewellers and the Sayoy Hotel. Left of centre is the Vines public house and, in the distance, St Luke's Church.

St George's Hall. c.1965. Taken when the hall was at its dirtiest after years of grime, dirt and pollution had taken its toll, the City Council decided that the money would be found to have it cleaned. On the left, at the end of the plateau, stands Professor Codman's world-famous Punch and Judy show, which has brought pleasure to children of all ages, from six to sixty. It originally stood in the middle of Lime Street, between Lime Street Station and the Washington Hotel. Owing to road changes it was moved to St George's Plateau. Interesting cars in the foreground include a Morris Oxford, a Ford Anglia, a Wolsey, a Morris Mini, a Ford Prefect and a Jaguar.

St George's Hall. c.1966. This rare photograph shows the Hall in the process of being cleaned. Not since it was officially opened had the public seen it so clean and, when completed, it looked superb. More cars in front are a Ford Zephyr Six, a Baby Austin, a Morris Minor van and a number of Minis.

Adelphi Hotel, Liverpool

3495

Adelphi Hotel. p.u.1908.
Situated in Lime Street between Brownlow Hill and Copperas Hill, the Adelphi is the most famous of all Liverpool's hotels. It was built by the London and Midland and Scottish Railway company on the site of an eighteenth-century coaching inn. The hotel was opened in 1913 and is now owned by the Britannia Group.

Adelphi Hotel. c.1970. This more modern photograph was taken after the façade was cleaned. Many famous people have stayed there, including royalty, film and theatre stars. At one time only the rich could afford to stay there but these days it is a bit more affordable. It was recently featured in the BBC series 'Hotel'. To the left of the hotel is the famous Vines public house and the Futurist Cinema.

Blacklers Stores. p.u.1915.
This must have been the best-loved department store in Liverpool; when it closed in 1988, tears were shed for its demise. It was said that "if you can't get it anywhere else, you will get it at Blacklers". I remember the rocking horse, the grottoes and the gigantic Father Christmas model which these days can be seen at the Albert Dock.

Blacklers Stores. c.1966.
Taken in December when Blacklers and many other department stores and city streets were profusely decorated during the festive season. Blacklers always had a good display inside and every store vied with each other to have the best grotto. The exterior decoration of Blacklers was not over-done, but I always remember the revolving orange ball on the corner of the store at the Elliot Street end. In nearby Clayton Square there were always three Christmas trees, donated by Denmark since the end of the second World War.

RANELAGH STREET. LIVERPOOL.

Ranalagh Street. c.1905. This rare photograph shows busy Ranalagh Street taken at the junction with Bold Street and Church Street. The Cheshire Lines Central Station is in front of the original Lewis's department store with, in the background, the old Adelphi Hotel. On the top left are: Great Charlotte Street; Cases Street; The Railway Hotel. Masons and Sweetmans were just two of the businesses on the left.

Bold Street. c.1905. The Lyceum Gentleman's Club is on the left. On its roof was a semaphore signalling device to receive messages from the Tower buildings at the Pier Head concerning the arrival of ships in the Mersey, so that their owners in the club could be informed. The Lyceum was built in 1803 and had a newsroom and library. Bold Street was always fashionable, with many fine houses built for the gentry. By the end of the 19th century, many of the ground floors were converted into fashionable shops. Off Bold Street, was Concert Street, named after the old Music Hall. At its rear are covered arches for patrons to alight from their sedan chairs without getting wet. At the top of Bold Street, St Luke's Church can just be seen in the distance.

BOLD STREET. LIVERPOOL.

St Luke's church. c.1928. Located at the junction of Bold Street, Berry Street and Leece Street, this beautiful church's foundation stone was laid in 1811 and it was consecrated in 1831. There is seating for 1,250 people and the tower contains a very fine peel of bells. The church was very badly damaged during the May blitz during the second World War. The bombed-out shell was saved from demolition when it was decided to retain it as a memorial to all those citizens who died during the war.

Church Street. c.1912. A view of church Street looking towards Lord Street and photographed at the junction with Ranalagh Street. Phillips the Jewellers can be seen on the right. This block has been partially redesigned as part of the new development for Clayton Square. On the left, the buildings protruding into Church Street were partially destroyed during the war and were eventually demolished to widen Church Street.

Church Street. p.u.1910. A superb sepia postcard showing the busy city centre, from the junction of Church Street, Paradise Street, Lord Street and Whitechapel known as "Holy Corner". Bunney's is on the left along with the Compton Hotel (now Marks & Spencers). Top right are the buildings previously mentioned that jutted out into Church Street. Who could forget Cooper's with that fresh aroma of ground coffee? In the middle of this junction is a Liverpool "Bobbie" – sometimes called a "Rozzer" or "Scuffer" – on point duty.

Church Street. c.1937. Looking in the opposite direction towards Lord Street. Paradise Street is to the left and Whitechapel to the right where we see the Refuge Assurance building above Horne Brothers. On the corner of Paradise Street are the "Don" stores. At the top are two trams nearing Derby Square and Castle Street.

Lord Street. p.u.1906.
An elevated view of
Lord Street taken from
Cooper's buildings. On the
left are the Don stores and
the building with the
arched windows was the
glass-covered Victorian
arcade. Other shops are
Edison's café, W. Jones the
dentists, Frisby Dykes and
the Bear's Paw restaurant.

Lord Street. p.u.1912. Left is
St George's Crescent, which
runs into Castle Street.
Half-way down, Lord Street
is bisected by North John
Street and South John Street.
There are various businesses
including the Boy Scout
outfitters, Frank Succs Ltd,
and Marine General Life
Assurance. It has always
been a very fashionable
street. Two trams trundle
along, loaded with shoppers,
and two more "Bobbies"
make up the picture.

Lord Street. p.u.1908.
Originally named Lord Molyneux Street, after Lord Molyneux, who had a family house at the top end on the north side. When the house was pulled down and replaced with fashionable shops, it was renamed Lord Street. St George's Crescent was named after St George's Church, constructed on the site of Liverpool Castle.

Queen Victoria monument. c.1906. An artist's impression of Derby Square, dominated by the Victoria Monument, which was built on the site of St George's Church. The foundation stone was laid by Earl Roberts in 1902 and it was unveiled by HRH Princess Louise on 27th September 1906. The artist has included the original Customs House and the Pier Head; the overhead railway is just visible.

Castle Street. p.u.1912. This fine photograph shows Castle Street from the Town Hall towards the Victoria Monument. This is the main commercial centre of the city, with many banks and offices. One of the main buildings is the Bank of England branch – a handsome Doric stone edifice. This establishment began its operations in Hanover Street in 1828 and moved to the present building in April 1849. The oldest relic in Castle Street is a sanctuary stone, first referred to in 1292. Fairs were held here and traders were protected from prosecution for a period of ten days before and after the fair.

Castle Street. p.u.1921. This impressive building at the end of Castle Street is Liverpool's Town Hall. It was designed by John Wood and built between 1749-1754. On top of the dome, the statue of Miniver looks down on the city. On the left at the junction of Castle Street and St James Street was the North and South Wales Bank, which has been recently refurbished and is now the Trials Restaurant and Hotel. On the right were Penlington and Batty, horologists and suppliers of chronometers to the Admiralty.

Royal Visit. c.1927. The lovely photograph on this postcard was taken on Liverpool Town Hall steps during one of many Royal visits to the city. Queen Mary poses for the press with the Lord Mayor and Lady Mayoress. The Royal party then continued down to the Pier Head to sail down the Mersey in order to open part of the Gladstone Dock.

Below: The scene outside the Town Hall, with King George V talking to the Liverpool City Police Chief Constable, whilst all the attention seems to be toward the mounted police officer and his horse. Queen Mary looks on from the steps. There are loads of top brass!

Exchange Flags. c.1910. At the rear of the Town Hall is a large square surrounded by tall office blocks. The square got its name from the fact that local merchants used to gather there to do business. The first buildings around the flags (i.e. the flag stones) were built at the end of the 18th century. Beneath one of the buildings, Derby House and under part of the flags, were the wartime headquarters in the fight against the threat of German U-boats attacking the Atlantic convoys. The Prime Minister, Winston Churchill stayed there on one of his visits.

Exchange Flags. c.1988. I wonder how many office workers who walk over the flags stop and think of the important events that took place beneath their feet. The buildings are the third to be built on the site and there are rumours that they are going to be replaced by new office blocks, as the present ones are not suitable for redevelopment.

Dale Street. c.1915. This artist-drawn postcard by Josh Fisher shows a lovely summer's day with the ladies in all their summer finery and the gentlemen in their lounge suits – yet the postcard reads 'A Happy Christmas'. On the right, just past Sir Thomas Street, are the Liverpool City Council Municipal Offices.

Dale Street. c.1910. Another view towards Hatton Gardens. Businesses on the left are "The City" hairdressing saloon, owned by G.F. Fletcher and advertising shaving at 2d and 4d for haircutting. Further down is Gresham Building, which consisted of shops and offices. At the junction with Hatton Gardens, were the City of Liverpool Magistrates Courts. Hatton Gardens also housed a Police Station and Liverpool Fire Brigade.

Exchange Station. c.1913. Situated in Tithebarn Street, it was built in 1850 for the Lancashire and Yorkshire Railway Company and opened on 13th May that year. The building closed as a station on 30th April 1977 to make way for the new Mersey-Rail system. All the lines and the platforms were removed but they retained the main part of the building. This photograph shows the magnificent façade of the building with the shops of R. Whittey, fishing tackle and sports goods and C. Francis, the confectioners.

Left: **St Nicholas's church. p.u.1902.** Heading down to the waterfront from Tithebarn Street into Chapel Street, to the Strand. On the corner is the beautiful church of St Nicholas.

Right: **St Nicholas's church. p.u.1905.** An artist's impression of St Nicholas's church viewed from the churchyard, with a mother and daughter enjoying the tranquillity there. These artist-drawn postcards with a greeting imprinted were very popular at the beginning of the century. The publishers spoilt the effect by showing a summer scene when a Christmas Greeting was included!

Exchange Station c.1978. This rare photograph shows the interior of Exchange Station, Tithebarn Street. Platforms 7 & 8 are prominent with the platform barriers, booking offices, destination boards, a stamping machine that would stamp out your name on a strip of aluminium, platform ticket machines and photographs of far-away places that one could only dream of going to, but which are commonplace these days.

From the Landing Stage. p.u.1907. This postcard shows part of the original tram terminus at the Pier Head. In front of St Nicholas' church is the Liverpool Overhead Railway and a line of hansom cabs await the next ship. To the right of the trams is the site for the Liver buildings. The old Tower building can be seen. Before looking at the next postcard, note the ladies in their summer dresses and the gentlemen in their lounge suits and the position of the trams and the hansom cabs.

Annie Garvey. c.1901. Another of Liverpool well-loved characters, Annie, was born, raised, lived and died in her little hut down at the Pier Head. The actual site of her home was at the side of the cornerstone at the entrance to the floating roadway, on the side that was later to be the bus station. It is not known how old she was when she died, but she was thought to have been 105.

Annie Garvey. c.1906. This is believed to be the last photograph to be taken of Annie outside her little hut at the Pier Head.

Annie Garvey,

[Reprinted from " Porcupine," May 19th, 1906]

Many happy returns of the day to Miss Annie Garvey, the maid of the George's Pier Head. Over her wealth of nut-brown hair, slightly tinged with grey, have passed one hundred and two winters. She is a living illustration of the medical dictum that every man is entitled to his century, and every woman to a little more. Her birthday was made memorable by the rebuilding of her wooden hut, a kind Roman Catholic priest having rendered her that inestimable service. She is now very comfortably housed, and is as proud of her new domicile as any German baron of his castle. Annie sells ha'porths of bread, marbles, toffee and matches to hawkers, newspaper boys, and other gutter merchants; and since PORCUPINE discovered her in June of last year her precarious income has been supplemented from time to time by pecuniary gifts.

**From the Landing Stage.
p.u.1908.** This is the same
photograph as the one on
page 27, except that the
publishers would not take
the trouble to take the same
view in the snow, so they
cheated by superimposing
snow on the original!

Floating Roadway. c.1901. The
floating roadway which
connected George's Dock gates
and the Landing Stage, was
open for 132 years and closed
in the 1980s. It was used to
convey vehicular traffic,
livestock and pedestrians to
the awaiting luggage boats,
ferries and liners. The floating
roadway was one of the most
famous landmarks in
Liverpool. When it was
reported in the press that it
was to be taken down, there
was a public outcry. But to no
avail – it was demolished and
part of a water treatment plant
was erected in its place. This
postcard shows a herd of sheep
being guided down to the
stage, followed by a laden
horse and cart.

LIVERPOOL *from the Air.*

Liverpool from the air. c.1930. This fine view of the Pier Head shows many landmarks, including Riverside Station, the Floating Stage and Roadway. The Liverpool Overhead Railway, Princes Dock, Pier Head Baths and Exchange Station all have gone; only St Nicholas' Church, the Liver Buildings, Cunard Buildings, the Mersey Docks and Harbour Company building and the White Star Line building survive.

Overhead Railway and New "LIVER" Offices. Water Street, LIVERPOOL

Liver Buildings. p.u.1910. The Liver Buildings were under construction in this postcard with the Liverpool Overhead Railway in front. To the left can just be seen the end of the Goree Piazzas, a block of warehouses based on a Venetian style. The Liver Buildings foundation stone was laid May 11th 1908 and the premises were opened by Lord Sheffield on 19th July 1911.

Pier Head. c.1952. An elevated view, showing in the foreground the Liverpool Overhead Railway heading south along the length of the docks. Beyond the Royal Liver buildings is the Cunard building and the ventilation shaft for the Mersey Tunnel. A large number of buses are moving to and from the bus station alongside the floating roadway. The Goree Piazzas are in what is now a wide dual carriageway along the dock road.

The Overhead Railway. c.1950. An Overhead Railway train has just pulled out of the Pier Head station and is just passing one of the ventilation shafts that serves the Mersey Tunnel; it is just about to cross James Street where, at one time, many types of transport crossed: the overhead railway, steam goods trains under the "Dockers' Umbrella", trams, buses, vehicular traffic and the underground railway which went from Liverpool to the Wirral. The advertisement on the steel girder arch bridge is for "Walkers' Falstaff".

Strand Street. p.u.1912. An early view taken from the overhead railway with a train which had been given the 'all clear' at the semaphore signal proceeding to the Customs House station. Strand Street is seen at a busy time with the carters and their teams outside the shops and warehouses plying their trade. The Goree piazzas, the overhead railway, shops and warehouses have all gone. On the right is Chevasse Park, due to be a Millennium Park in the year 2000. Beyond the warehouses, the roof of the White Star Line offices can just be seen.

Looking South. c.1930. This is a superb view taken from an elevated position, looking along part of the overhead railway towards James Street and Customs House stations. The Goree piazzas, White Star building, Customs House, Hydraulic Pumping Station, the Anglican Cathedral (in the course of construction) and Canning Dock are all visible in this lovely postcard.

Birdseye View of Liverpool (South).
Overhead Railway, Strand Street and Docks.

Oceanic Hotel. c.1987. We come from the docks to Duke Street. In the early 18th century many fine houses were built here, one being converted into a public house, "The Monro". On the corner of Duke Street and Slater Street, No.105, is an impressive office building, the Union News Room – Liverpool's first Public Library and Museum. Further up, the derelict building at the corner of Colquitt Street was the Oceanic Hotel, used by emigrants to "The New World" prior to embarking on a sailing ship for America, Canada, or Australia. There have been plans to restore the building as a hotel or museum. Behind it are the last of the back-to-back houses.

Roll of Honour. c.1925. This is a photograph of one of about 400 white vellum leaves which were produced by a London artist and are to be bound together and placed in the Cathedral war memorial. The colouring on every leaf is superb and every leaf is different. The one shown carries the King's signature. One of the pages is to Lord Kitchener and the design is magnificent. He was a Freeman of the City of Liverpool and that is why he is included in the memorial. All the leaves were on display to the public at the Basnett Gallery, Liverpool.

THEY WHOM THIS VOLUME COMMEMORATES were numbered among those who, at the call of King and Country, left all that was dear to them, endured hardness, faced danger, and finally passed out of the sight of men by the path of duty and self sacrifice, giving up their own lives that others might live in freedom.

Let those who come after see to it that their name be not forgotten.

George R.I.

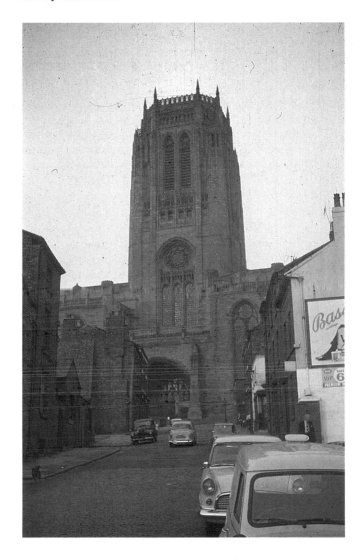

Left: **The Anglican Cathedral. c.1965.** A rare photograph of the partially-constructed cathedral, taken from Washington Street, which ran from Great George Street to St James Street. On a clear day the view from the top of the cathedral tower is unrivalled. It offers a 360-degree view of the city and suburbs, Wirral and North Wales. Building work began on the cathedral in 1904 and it was completed in October 1978. The architect was Sir Giles Gilbert Scott – a Catholic. He was 21 years of age when his design was accepted.
Right: **The Anglican Cathedral. c. 1966.** Another view of the nearly-completed cathedral taken from Gambia Terrace near Hope Street, near to its junction with Upper Duke Street and Canning Street.

Pitt Street. c.1920. It was named after William Pitt the Elder, who was the 1st Earl of Chatham and Prime Minister in 1756. The Upper Frederick Street area was overcrowded, with disease-ridden yards and slum dwellings known as 'courts'. With its proximity to the docks there were many East and West African immigrants but, in the 19th century, Pitt Street became the centre of Europe's "China Town". It was during the late 1820s that the Chinese started to settle there. This postcard shows one of the blocks beautifully decorated for this special occasion.

Park Road. c.1905. Heading out to the suburbs, we travel along Park Road. On the left is the entrance to the booking office of Dingle Station, the southern terminus for the Liverpool Overhead Railway. The station was unusual, as passengers went 'down' to an 'overhead' station. The building was demolished when the L.O.R. closed in 1956. The site is now occupied by a garage, although the slope down to the station tunnel is still there along with its white tiled lining. On a recent visit, there was still that musty smell associated with an underground railway. Opposite the entrance is the ancient Toxteth Chapel, just visible in the photograph.

Bryant and May. c.1987.
The Bryant and May factory as built in 1920 for McQuire Patterson and Palmer, matchmakers. Before moving to Garston their factory was in Lightbody Street, Vauxhall, Liverpool. This photograph was taken outside the factory's office block in 1987 to promote the new vehicle liveries, for Swan Vestas and England's Glory matches.

Bryant and May. c.1983. HRH Princess Margaret paid a visit to the factory on 20th April 1983. She was photographed being accompanied by William Archibald, the General Manager, in the 'match hall'. She was presented with monogrammed book matches and a silver matchbox, suitably inscribed. Limited edition boxes of Cooks' matches with special labels were issued to factory workers, to commemorate the visit. The factory closed and became the property of the Swedish Match Company in 1994. It was converted in part into a film studio which is becoming increasingly popular with film and television companies.

Liverpool Airport. c.1950. Situated at Speke on the outskirts of Liverpool, the airport was opened in 1933 by Liverpool City Council. The original airport used a farmhouse as a control centre and terminal building. Imperial Airways began its Liverpool – Manchester – Birmingham – Croydon service, but it only lasted for three months. In July 1933 the airport was officially opened by the Marquis of Londonderry, Secretary of State for Air. Although grossly underused, this is a fine airport and there are plans to bring it up to the standard of other regional airports. This is a photograph taken of the airport control tower which, in its day was the most sophisticated in the north of England. It was taken from the spectators' gallery, very close to the airport apron and control tower. Increased security has made it necessary to keep spectators well away from the aircraft.

Liverpool Airport. c 1964. A Cambrian Airways Viscount V701 aircraft, G-AMOL has just landed at Speke after its flight from London. On board were the "Searchers" pop group, namely Mike Pender, John McNally, Tony Jackson and Chris Curtis. Many airlines have used Speke, including Cambrian, British Eagle, BEA, Air Lingus, Manx and British Midland. Notice how close the spectators are to the aircraft.

CONCORDE at LIVERPOOL AIRPORT   WPC 82

Liverpool International Airport. c.1993. A British Airways Concorde G-BOAG stands on the apron at Liverpool's International Airport being refuelled ready to fly off to London Heathrow via the Grand National course at Aintree. Concorde is the only commercial supersonic aircraft in regular service in the world and it has been flown by Air France and British Airways since 1976. This Anglo-French project began in 1962.

Liverpool International Airport. c.1993. The Merseyside Police helicopter, outside its hanger in its original livery – since changed to all black. It is an Aerospatiale A5.355 Twin Squirrel, registration G-BOOV, with twin gas-turbines, a maximum speed of 140 knots and 3 hours endurance. It is fitted with "Nitesun" and "Skyshout" systems. The helicopter is a integral part of a first-class police force and plays its part in reducing the crime rate and bringing the perpetrators to justice. It has a crew of one pilot and two police officers.

Speke Hall. c. 1968. Situated between the now disused Speke Airport and the modern international airport, is this beautiful half-timbered Tudor house. Built for the Norris family, who were staunch Catholics, it was completed in 1598, and within its walls they had built their own chapel. Also constructed was a 'priest's hole' used when a local priest needed to be hidden from persecution. It is owned by the National Trust, and makes for an excellent day out for all the family, as this picture shows.

The River and its shipping

Map of the River Mersey. c.1911. This was issued by the Cadbury's chocolate company and was used in schools as a reward card for good attendance or good work. The map shows the source of the Mersey in Derbyshire and sees it wind its way down through Stockport, past Lymm and Runcorn and into the Mersey as we know it.

Transporter Bridge. c.1911. This was built in 1905 to replace the original ferry crossing between Widnes and Runcorn. Pedestrians could use the ferry or walk over the river on a foot-walk alongside the railway bridge. With increasing traffic, plans were laid for an alternative one. This too became inadequate and an impressive new bridge was built alongside the railway bridge. This was opened in 1951 and the old transporter bridge was demolished.

STALBRIDGE LOCK & DOCK, GARSTON

Stalybridge Dock. c.1914. In Garston as early as 1793 a small inlet was used as a salt dock, where manufacturing of this commodity was undertaken by Thomas Blackburn. Stalybridge Dock was built in 1909 and is named after the chairman of the London and North Western Railway Company, who had the dock built after taking over the St Helens Canal and Railway Company. In the course of construction of the dock, Garston lost Castle Street and the Mersey Hotel. This postcard shows Elders' and Fyffes' banana boat "Manistee", which was built in 1910 and sunk in 1941. The other vessel is not known but it flies the Norwegian flag.

Garston Old Dock. c.1915. The first dock – the "old" dock – was constructed under an Act of 1846. It is believed to have been built in the early 1850s by the St Helens Canal and Railway Company. The second dock –"North"– was built in 1876. These docks were used for the importation of bananas, timber, chemicals, ore and for the export of coal to Ireland.

Cressington Promenade. c.1918.
This gives fine views over the Mersey and to North Wales. At its southern end are Garston Docks and, as seen on this card, the northern end is connected to Otterspool Promenade. This was the Liverpool Corporation refuse tip, since reclaimed and landscaped. Cressington and Grassendale railway stations formed part of Wood End Park, a private residential estate. It was developed in the 1860s and the railway station opened in 1873. In Victorian times, this was where the 'Upper Crust' of society lived and where the infamous "Maybrick" murder was committed. Members of Parliament, ship owners, solicitors, merchants and ships' captains lived in the area.

Dingle Oil Terminal. c.1930.
In 1919, bunkering facilities were provided at Dingle Bank, on Mersey Docks and Harbour Board land. The first oil company to be established there was the Anglo-American Oil Company. The Dingle Oil Terminal was connected to Herculaneum Dock by means of two 3,000-foot lengths of 10-inch diameter pipe-work through which fuel oil could be pumped to ships berthed at the terminal or to railway wagons. In 1923 a river jetty was built to accommodate oil and petroleum.

Harrington and Herculaneum Docks. c.1980. This view was taken after the old docks had closed and the area had been redeveloped and revitalised after a number of years in dereliction. The docks were filled in, the old dock sheds refurbished and made into a business park. Part of the Dingle and Toxteth docks were used for the Liverpool Garden Festival which ran from 2nd May to 14th October 1984.

Liverpool Overhead Railway. c. 1990. The overhead railway ran from Seaforth to the Dingle. It ran parallel with the docks and the River Mersey for almost its entire length. It deviated away from the docks after leaving Brunswick and veered left until it disappeared into the tunnel, which took it into the terminus at Dingle Station. This photograph shows the preserved L.O.R. tunnel entrance. It was cleaned in time for the Garden Festival in 1984.

Brunswick Dock. p.u.1938.

Brunswick Dock was next to Coburg Dock. It opened in 1832 for the discharge of grain to the silos using pneumatic elevators. In 1932, further elevators were built on the north-east quay to ship grain to the Coburg granary. Ropner Shipping Company's tramp steamer, *Ullapool,* is seen discharging here. In 1941, loaded with grain, she hit a mine and sank in the Mersey off Birkenhead. As the water reached the grain it expanded; she split in two and was not salvaged from her position over the Queensway Tunnel until after the war. The two silos have been demolished and the warehouses converted into a business park. Coburg Dock is now a superb marina with many small boats and yachts.

The Dock Road. c.1980. This modern photograph is included to show how the area has been developed from derelict dock land to a thriving business and leisure complex. It was photographed from the fourth floor of a dock road office block. Behind it is Wapping Basin and, beside the Wapping Dock, the ex-Wapping bonded warehouse which has been converted into luxury apartments. To the right is the main car park for the Albert Dock shopping centre. The car park was built on the site of Dukes Dock and Kings Nos.1 and 2 docks. The large building in the course of construction is the new Custom and Excise Headquarters.

RMS Mauretania. c.1938.
Photographed at Rock Ferry looking towards the Cammell Laird shipyard at Birkenhead. On the slip-way in the course of construction is the Cunard liner *RMS Mauretania* shortly before her launch on 28th July 1938. The 'Mauri' as she was affectionately known, began her maiden voyage from Liverpool to New York on 17th June 1939. In March 1940 she was requisitioned as a troopship and made 48 voyages, carrying over 350,000 personnel. After an overhaul and refit at Birkenhead, she resumed service in 1947 on the Liverpool-New York route, before being transferred to Southampton. In 1965 she was sold to Thomas Ward and broken up at Inverkeithing, Scotland in 1966.

The Floating Dock. c.1912. In its time, this was the world's largest floating dock and it was built for the Admiralty at Birkenhead in 1912. It left its dock at Cammell Laird's on 14th August towed by 10 tugs, including *Blackcock*, brought in to assist in manoeuvring it out of the dock. It weighed 49,000 tons and had a lifting capacity of 32,000 tons. She was 680 feet long and 144 feet wide. She had eight powerful steam-driven capstans, made by Hadfield and company, for warping ships into position. She is seen here at on trial in Portmouth with the Super dreadnought *HMS Monarch*.

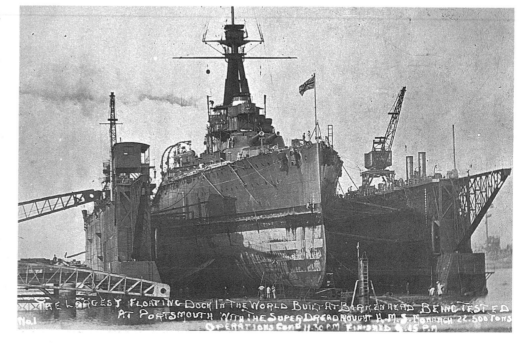

HMS Ark Royal. c.1955.
The fourth *Ark Royal* was built at Cammell Laird's, on the same stocks as its predecessor. It was planned that she should carry about 100 aircraft. The cost of the new *Ark Royal* was estimated to exceed £3,000,000. She was launched by Her Majesty Queen Elizabeth II in 1955.

Salt House Dock. c.1930.
This dock is now part of the Albert Dock Complex. It was originally built by Jessie Hartley, a dock engineer, and the Albert Dock was opened by Prince Albert. It was built on the site of an old salt house, hence this dock's name. In the right foreground is one of the sailing barges. To the left is part of the Albert Dock offices, now used as the Granada News studio. Behind the barge is an ex-naval vessel, the British Protection vessel *HMS Eagle* an ex-Man of War.

HMS Thetis. c.1939. The vessel was lying on the seabed 14 miles off Great Orme Head. It was eventually lifted and towed to Moelfre, Anglesey where she was beached, as the photograph shows. A small boat has just pulled alongside, possibly with Board of Trade officials on board.

HMS Thetis. c.1939. The *Thetis* tragedy was one of the worst accidents involving both civilian and naval personnel. This submarine was built at Cammell Laird's and, during her sea trials, she sank in Liverpool Bay. Ninety-nine lives were lost. This is a photograph of the memorial to all those brave men who died.

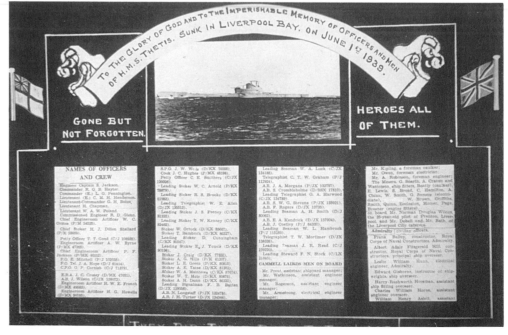

The Mammoth. c.1939.
This crane, with a lifting capacity of 200 tons, was a familiar site on the Mersey for many years. It was built by a Dutch firm, originally for the Russians. After the revolution, it was no longer required by Russia and it was offered to the British Government and purchased by the Mersey Docks and Harbour Board in 1920. It left the Mersey for the last time in 1986, having been sold to a Scandinavian Company. She is seen here with tugs of the Alexander Towing Company.

HMS Eagle. c.1930. At the end of her war service, this fine vessel was brought to Liverpool and berthed in front of the Customs House in Salt House Dock. She was converted into an officer training ship. Additional accommodation was added in the form of an extra deck but she still retained her masts and original black and white colouring.

Canning Dock. p.u.1909. A superb photograph by Wright and Co, Bootle. In the background is The Mersey Docks and Harbour Board building with, to its right, part of the hydraulic pumping station and, to its left, what was known as "Little Nova Scotia" on Mann Island. It was so-named for the immigrant sail makers that lived and worked there. Front centre is the sailing barge, *Lucy*, beautifully reflected in the dock.

HMS Eagle. c.1931. As seen by this photograph, her masts have been removed and she was repainted in brown. All of her remaining guns were removed and were replaced by windows. She was renamed *HMS Eaglet*. While in Salt House Dock she caught fire and was totally destroyed. Behind her in the photograph is the original Customs House which was bombed during the war and eventually demolished.

Bar Lightships. c.1960. The tug *Hazelgarth* is seen mid-river having passed the Brunswick and Coburg docks and just passing the Albert Dock. The first lightship in tow is the *Alarm* which was replaced by the *Planet*; the second lightship is unknown.

The Albert Dock c.1990.
Photographed from the roof of Merseyside Police H.Q. Canning Place, looking towards the Mersey. In the foreground is the Salt House Dock with the Albert Dock which has been transformed from dereliction to a thriving tourist attraction with shops, cafés, restaurants, the Merseyside Maritime Museum, a studio, offices and luxury apartments. The columned building was a dock office and is now the Granada Television Newsroom and studio. It was built by Jessie Hartley. The columns, entablature and pediment are all of cast iron.

The Tram Terminus.
p.u.1907. Standing majestically at the Pier Head is the HQ of the Mersey Docks and Harbour Board. To its right can just be seen the masts of the sailing ships berthed at the Albert Dock. In the foreground is the Pier Head tram and later the bus station, with three tram. They were owned and run by Liverpool Corporation Tramways. Some of the advertisements on the trams are for "Horlicks Malted Milk", "Jacob's Cream Crackers" and "Van Houton's Cocoa". The family in their long winter coats hurry down towards the ferries.

**The Liver Buildings.
p.u.1914.** Although this
postcard was sent through
the post in 1914, I think that
the photograph was taken
about the same time as the
previous one. The Liver
Buildings were built between
1908-1911, and opened by
Lord Sheffied on 19th July.
Just behind can be seen the
original Tower Buildings
and, to the left, part of the
Pier Head swimming baths
are visible.

**Royal Yacht Britannia.
c.1988.** This photograph,
taken by the author on a hot
summer's day at the Pier
Head, on one of the first
visits of the royal yacht to the
city. She was last here on
30th October 1997 on her
final tour prior to being
de-commissioned. It was
decided that she was to
spend the rest of her days as
a tourist attraction and
conference centre at Leith, in
Scotland.

The Liver Buildings. p.u.1912. A rare photograph taken from the St George's Landing Stage at the exit from the floating roadway at high tide. A solitary heavily-laden hand cart with a lady walking behind it, is approaching the stage. The Liver Buildings clock shows almost 4.40 and, by the lack of activity, I would say that it is early morning. One of the waiting rooms can be seen at the tram terminus.

Pier Head. c.1990. The Royal Liver buildings make a perfect backdrop for this postcard of the Merseyside Police Mounted Department, wearing ceremonial uniform. The police officers are, left to right: Chief Inspector P. Ferguson, Constable S. Fry and Constable P. Letford. The horses' names are not known.

Pier Head vista. c.1930. Another aerial view of the waterfront, but this time looking south from Princes Half-Tide as far as Brunswick Dock. From the bottom left, Liverpool Overhead Railway snakes its way parallel with the river, towards its terminus at the Dingle Station. Some buildings that are no longer with us can just be seen: The Sailors' Home; Canning Place; The Customs House; Church House; Riverside Station.

Royal Visit. c.1913. On one of the many Royal visits to the city, we were graced by the presence of their Majesties King George V and Queen Mary. One of their duties was to open the first phase of Gladstone Dock, Bootle. Instead of travelling to Bootle by Royal car, they went by boat. They boarded the Mersey Docks and Harbour Board tender, *Galatea* and sailed up the river to view the docks on route. The *Galatea* is seen leaving the landing stage en-route to Gladstone Dock with the Royal Party on board.

Royal Visit. c.1913. This photograph was taken on board the *Galatea* by Wright & Co. of Bootle, one of the few photographers who had permission to board the vessel and take official photographs of the visit. The Royal party is seen on the bridge of the *Galatea* along with Royal Navy personnel and the tender's crew - a proud moment for them.

The Landing Stage. c.1912. An early view of the St George's landing stage with a mixed bunch of people. Some are watching the ships on the river, some just strolling along, others are waiting for the ferry. The only vessel on the river at this time is a sailing barge trying to catch the wind.

The Landing Stage. c.1907.
Many famous ships have
visited the Mersey, some
never to return. To others it
was their home port. Tied-up
at the stage is the White Star
Line vessel, the *Cedric*, built
by Harland and Wolff,
Belfast in 1903, for the
White Star's Liverpool to
New York service. Her
maiden voyage was on 11th
February 1903. She was
converted to Armed
Merchant Cruiser in
November 1914. At the back
of the stage the Dock Board
offices are in the course of
construction.

Christmas Greetings. c.1910.
Wright & Co of Bootle
produced many superb
postcards, many of them
shipping cards. They also
produced Christmas
Greetings postcards, like this
one. The photographer,
William Thomas Wright took
two of his own photographs
and set them on a Christmas
Greeting background and
re-photographed them to
produce this card. The ship
on the left is the White Star
Line ship, *The Laurentic*,
berthed at the stage. The
other is of pigs being
unloaded from a luggage boat
which carried livestock and
transport across the Mersey.

The busy Mersey. p.u.1908.
Photographed by Wright &
Co, Bootle from the Landing
Stage and showing great
activity on the river. Sixteen
ships are shown, including
the paddle steamer, *Queen
Victoria*, the *Cedric* owned by
the White Star Line and the
Empress of Britain owned by
Canadian Pacific. Other
vessels include tugs, ferries,
gig boats and yachts. In all, a
stunning photographic
postcard.

Princes Dock. c.1920. An
elevated view of the Princes
Dock and, from the right: the
Overhead Railway; Princes
Dock warehouses; Waterloo
Dock warehouses (which
have been converted into
luxury flats); Princes Graving
Dock; the Belfast ferry;
Riverside Station and, in the
distance, New Brighton
Tower.

"LUSITANIA"

***RMS Lusitania* at the Stage. c.1908.**
This majestic Cunard Line ship, seen
in this rare postcard shot, tied up at
the stage and being prepared for
another voyage across the Atlantic.
A conveyor is loading supplies onto
her while two Liverpudlians watch
what is going on. Two more lean
against hand carts.

The busy Mersey. c.1909.
Another busy scene with the *Lusitania* berthed at the stage after completing another transatlantic voyage. Three tugs which assisted her have also tied up. The Cunard tender, *Skirmisher*, is just pulling alongside, just seen behind a ferry. Another ferry has just left the crowded stage for Birkenhead loaded to the gunnels with passengers. In the background is Riverside Station.

Luggage Room. c.1950. After the passengers had disembarked from their ship, they collected their baggage from the Baggage Room where it was examined. The sign says "Mersey Docks and Harbour Board. Prince Landing Stage, Baggage Examining Room" Notice hanging from the roof the old style gas heaters. There is a "Cook's Tours" kiosk also.

Customs Hall. c.1951. This crowded scene is the customs hall, with Customs officers somehow managing to sort out what appears to be a complete jumble. Most of the passengers are West African immigrants, along with regular passengers.

Princes Parade. c.1910. After docking and when the passengers had cleared Customs, they made their way to Princes Parade where they either took horse-drawn coaches to hotels or railway stations, or into Riverside Station to continue their journey onto London. In the far left of this postcard a funnel of one of the liners is visible. Also in the picture is a Hansom cab.

Princes Parade. c.1960. The lovely canopied structure over Princes Parade was partially destroyed during the war and was later demolished. Although the canopy of the arched wall has gone, the wall remains as a small reminder of those halcyon days.

Princes Parade. c.1910. Another view of the covered section of Princes Parade, showing its height and length. It was ideal for keeping passengers dry from the rain and away from the wind. On the right is the wall of Riverside Station and on the left the archways leading down to the gangways to the stage. A horse-drawn cab is heading along with a fare, while a family walks towards the gangways with the driver of the horse-drawn cab.

Princes Parade. c.1968. This photograph was taken in almost the same position as the previous one, except that the covered section has gone, leaving the wall on the right of Riverside Station. On the left is an electricity sub-station and, further down, is the shell of the luggage rooms and, in the distance, the walled arches. At the far end of what was Riverside Station is the shore-based *HMS Eaglet*.

Riverside Station. c.1905. Opened in 1895 and built adjacent to the north end of the Landing Stage, giving easy access for passengers before and after a voyage across the Atlantic. Express trains left Riverside Station and wound their way slowly through the dock estate, alongside Waterloo Dock Warehouse, and across Waterloo Road (the dock road). The trains then entered the Waterloo Tunnel, travelling under the city centre and finally emerging at Edge Hill Station where they continued on their way to London.

Riverside Railway Station. LIVERPOOL.

Princes Parade. c.1976. This bare view shows the remains of Riverside Station, Princes Parade, with the luggage and baggage halls and the covered arch. While a John Lennon Memorial concert took place in 1975 at Pier Head, a temporary bus station was established at Riverside. Unfortunately, the archways in one of the side walls were not big enough for a bus to pass under, so the side wall was demolished. After the concert, the Riverside site was abandoned and buses returned to Pier Head.

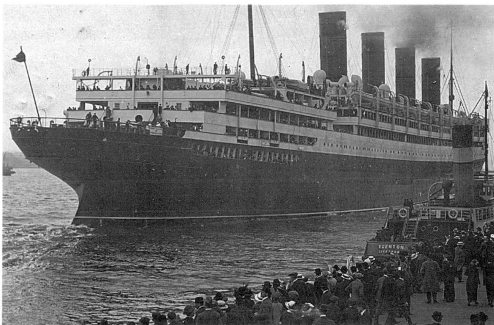

Maiden Voyage. p.u.1915. The Cunarder, *Aquitania*, leaves a crowded stage on her maiden voyage, May 30th 1914, from Liverpool to Queenstown and New York. She was built by John Brown & Co, Glasgow and was the last ship to be built with four funnels. She had four screws with four direct-acting steam turbines. She ended her days when she was sold and broken up at Garloch, Scotland in 1950.

RMS Lusitania. c.1909.
Another rare photographic postcard of the *Lusitania* which, like those of the *Titanic*, are becoming more and more collectable. She is seen anchored mid-river after another voyage. On 7th May 1915, she was torpedoed by the German submarine U-20 off the Old Head of Kinsale, Southern Ireland and sank with the loss of 1,198 lives.

Lusitania **Medal. p.u.1917.**
An unusual coloured postcard claiming a German Victory. This medal has been struck in Germany to commemorate the most glorious achievement of the German navy in deliberately destroying an unarmed passenger ship together with 1,198 non-combatants, men, women and children. This postcard brought an angry response from the British Government when it was published.

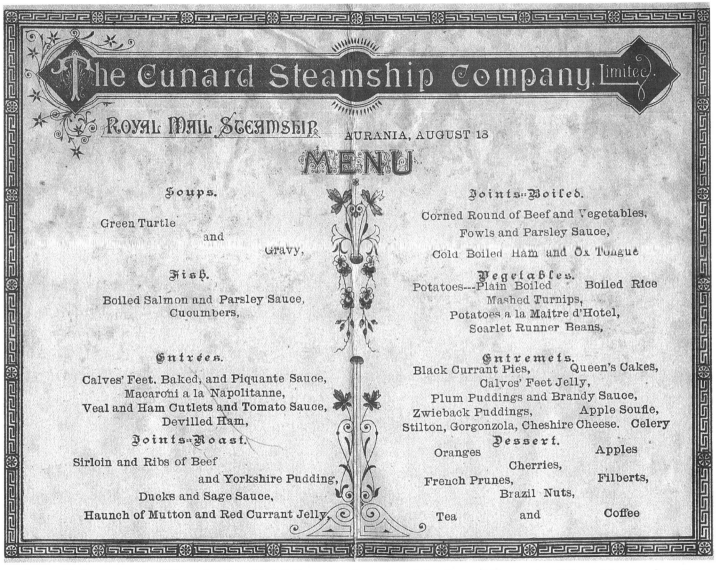

The Cunard Steamship Company, Limited.

Royal Mail Steamship

AURANIA, AUGUST 13

MENU

Soups.

Green Turtle

and

Gravy,

Fish.

Boiled Salmon and Parsley Sauce,
Cucumbers,

Entrées.

Calves' Feet, Baked, and Piquante Sauce,
Macaroni a la Napolitanne,
Veal and Ham Cutlets and Tomato Sauce,
Devilled Ham,

Joints—Roast.

Sirloin and Ribs of Beef
and Yorkshire Pudding,
Ducks and Sage Sauce,
Haunch of Mutton and Red Currant Jelly,

Joints—Boiled.

Corned Round of Beef and Vegetables,
Fowls and Parsley Sauce,
Cold Boiled Ham and Ox Tongue

Vegetables.

Potatoes---Plain Boiled   Boiled Rice
Mashed Turnips,
Potatoes a la Maitre d'Hotel,
Scarlet Runner Beans,

Entremets.

Black Currant Pies,   Queen's Cakes,
Calves' Feet Jelly,
Plum Puddings and Brandy Sauce,
Zwieback Puddings,   Apple Soufle,
Stilton, Gorgonzola, Cheshire Cheese.   Celery

Dessert.

Oranges   Apples
Cherries,
French Prunes,   Filberts,
Brazil Nuts,

Tea   and   Coffee

Cunard Menu. c.1887. When the Royal Mail Steamer, *Aurania*, of the Cunard line, set sail from Liverpool on its Atlantic service, the first-class passengers sat down to what is shown here. The menu was given out on 18th August 1887. What a fine feast to tickle one's palate. On the front of the menu was a lithograph drawing of the *Aurania* along with details of interest to the passengers. It lists all the Cunard agencies, plus leading hotels, including the Adelphi, Liverpool, whose manager at the time was W. Ludlow. On the back is a list of Cunard's fleet on the Atlantic and Mediterranean services, plus advertisements.

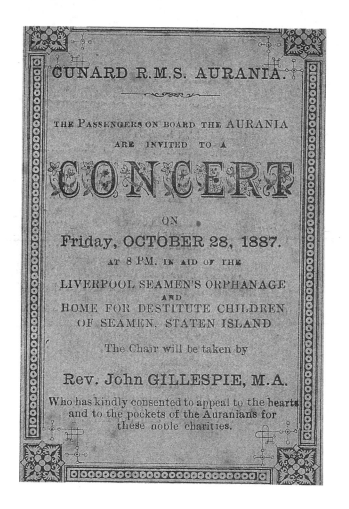

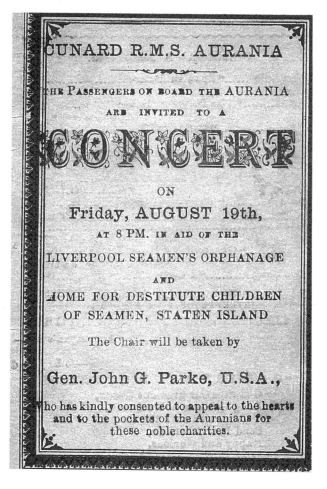

Concert Programmes. c.1887. To help while away the Atlantic voyage, a varied amount of entertainment was provided on board. These two programmes show what was to be enjoyed by the passengers. This Concert was in aid of the Liverpool Seamen's Orphanage and the Home for Destitute Children of Seamen, Staten Island, America. The Chairman was a Gen. John G. Parke, USA, who kindly consented to appeal to the hearts and to the pockets of the "Auranians" for these noble charities.

MV Britannic. c.1935.
A regular visitor to the Mersey and much loved by all those from Liverpool. She was built by Harland & Wolff, Belfast for the White Star Line. Her 27-foot forward funnel was a dummy – it housed water tanks and an engineers' smoking room. She remained in profitable service across the Atlantic, alternating with cruising in the winter months, until requisitioned as a troopship in 1939. She survived the war unscathed and, after a major refit, returned to Cunard in May 1948. Cunard sold her in November 1960 to Wards Shipbreakers, Inverkeithing: the last of the White Star Liners.

Training Ships. c.1910.
Photographed by Wright & Co, Bootle – three training ships anchored mid-river for many years. From left: the *Conway*, built in 1822 as the *Winchester*, a sixty-gun frigate. Renamed in 1862 at the end of her fighting days, she was anchored in the Mersey and used as an officer training ship. Whilst being towed through the Menai Straits she broke her tow and ran aground, caught fire and was destroyed. The *Akbar*, a reformatory ship, was built in 1801 as a thirty-eight gun frigate, the *Cornwallis*. The *Indefatigable*, known as the 'Indi', was built in 1848. While anchored in the Mersey, she catered for orphans and children in poor circumstances.

The *Vigilant*. c.1906.
Owned by the Mersey Docks and Harbour Board and built in Glasgow in 1903. This salvage ship served the River Mersey for many years. In 1952 she was renamed *Steadfast* and sold for scrap to Dublin in 1954.

Princes Half-Tide Dock. p.u.1913. Taken from the end of the St George's Landing Stage, with a family enjoying the sea breezes. To the right is one of the Waterloo Dock warehouses. This is the one that was destroyed in the war. The other, not seen in this picture, has been renovated and converted into luxury apartments. The square tower, designed by Jessie Hartley, was part of the original Liverpool Observatory, later transferred to Bidston on the Wirral. A Mersey 'Flat' sailing barge is just leaving the Half-Tide dock entrance while another is making its way out of the Mersey. The Half-Tide entrance and dock were built in 1821.

The *Applegarth*. c.1959. On the evening of 13th January 1960, a Rea Towing Company tug, the *Applegarth*, collided with the 10,000-ton Scottish Shire Line freighter, *Perthshire*. Along with the tugs, *Throstlegarth* and *Langarth*, it was assisting the freighter into the outer basin at Birkenhead. The *Applegarth* got into difficulties, listed slightly to port, rolled over, came out on the starboard side and sank within seconds. Only one member of the crew, Ernest Perry, was picked up but died as the crew of the *Throstlegarth* tried to revive him. The photograph shows the *Applegarth* assisting a Blue Funnel Line vessel into Birkenhead Docks. The crew member seen at the stern is John Childs – one of those who died in the tragedy.

The *Applegarth*. c.1960. This sad photograph shows the salvaged wreck of the Rea tug, the *Applegarth*, not long after she had been brought to the surface after the terrible tragedy. The bodies of all the crew were recovered from the wreck. Those that died were: Captain Leslie Fenby, Mathew Turton, Derek Hughes, Ernest Duncalf, John Childs, John Dolphin and Ernest Perry. After a complete refit, the *Applegarth* returned to the Rea Towing Company's fleet, to be commanded by her skipper Captain Alf Brown who missed the fatal collision as he was ill at the time.

Fishing boat. p.u.1906. A very nice photographic postcard of one of the many fishing boats based on the Mersey. To the right of this boat is one of the sailing barges that plied its trade in the river. A merchant ship is starting another voyage, while a liner has just arrived from another transatlantic voyage.

THE SANDON DOCK ENTRANCES, LIVERPOOL

Sandon Docks. c.1921. This aerial postcard photograph shows the Sandon Half-Tide entrance locks. The Cunard liner, Carmania, is in the basin and other vessels include Cunard Mediterranean refrigeration ships. On the far left, in Huskisson Branch No. 2 is the twin-funnelled *RMS Aruba* and in the Cunard berth at Huskisson No.1, is the *Kaiserin Auguste Victoria*, on loan to Cunard for six voyages.

RMS Oceanic. **c.1900.** The White Star Line, *Oceanic,* about to embark on another voyage. She was built by Harland & Wolff, Belfast in 1899. In 1901 she collided with and sank the Waterford coaster, *Kilcora,* off Tuskar with the loss of seven lives. In 1902, White Star were absorbed into the International Mercantile Marine Co. owned by J. Pierpoint Morgan. In 1905 there was a mutiny on board and in 1914 she became an Armed Merchant Cruiser. She ran onto rocks a month later off Foula, Jutland, and sank – no lives lost.

RMS Saxonia. p.u.1906. This beautiful Cunarder, sister ship to the *Ivernia*, was photographed by Wright & Co, Bootle, assisted by two Rea tugs into her berth at Huskisson Dock. Built in 1900 by John Brown & Company, Glasgow, she had the tallest funnel of any ship in the world. Her maiden voyage was from Liverpool to Queenstown (City of Cobh, now Cork) to Boston on 22nd May 1900. She was used on winter cruises from New York to the Mediterranean. At the start of the First World War she saw service as a troopship and as a German prisoner-of-war ship moored on the River Thames. From 1920-1925 she was on the Hamburg - New York service. In 1925 she was sold and broken up in Holland.

RMS Mauretania. p.u.1908. Built by Swan Hunter and Wigham Richardson at Wallsend on Tyne. She was launched on 20th September 1906 and completed in October 1907. Her maiden voyage was on 16th November from Liverpool - Queenstown - New York; she broke the eastbound Blue Ribband record in a time of four days, 22 hours and 29 minutes. She was photographed on her way into Sandon Dock, after passing through Sandon Half-Tide entrance.

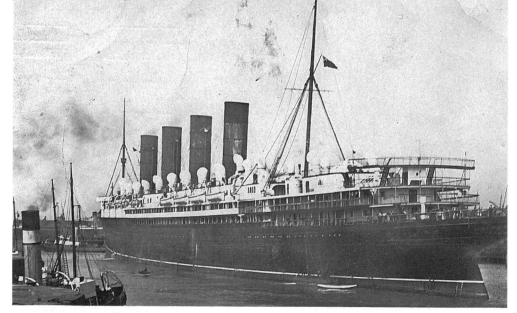

Ocean Monarchs. p.u.1909.
The *Mauretania* and
Lusitania photographed in
Canada Dock, Basin, Bootle
on 14th October 1909. The
three tugs in attendance are,
left to right:
Alexander, built in 1906; the
Hornby, built in 1908; the
Trafalgar built in 1906. Two
gig boats complete the
picture. The *Mauretania* was
named after the Roman name
for Morocco and the
Lusitania was named after
Roman Portugal.

Hazelgarth. c.1961. Another
view of the *Hazelgarth*, one
of Rea's tugs. She is seen
waiting her turn to enter
Langton River entrance. She
was built by P.K. Harrison of
Appledore and had a 1600hp
engine. After many years
faithful service, she was sold
to another tug company in
December 1988. On the right
is the tug, *John Lamey* with a
Smith-Coggins crane in tow
and, on the left, is the Shell
bunkering boat, *Perso*. Two
other tugs are seen heading
up towards the lock gates.

The *RMS Lusitania*. c.1909.
An unusual view of this beautiful ship, laid up in the Canada Graving Dock. Until one sees her in dry dock you do not realise how big she really was and how much was below the waterline. She is gigantic compared with the dockers on the quayside and those standing at the bottom of the dry dock.

Brocklebank Dock. p.u.1902.
An early postcard of
Brocklebank Dock, Bootle, on
30th October 1902. It is
crowded with sailing ships
and not a funnel in sight.
The steam barge on the right,
carrying a cargo of rope, is
similar to those owned by
D.W. Williams. The postcard
was published by Bunneys
Ltd, the well-known
Liverpool department store,
sadly no longer with us.

Langton Dock. c.1908. A
busy day at the Langton
Dock, Bootle. In the centre
is the hydraulic pumping
station that assisted with
the opening and closing of
the lock gates. The
pump-house keeper, a Mr.
Petrie, lived there with his
wife. Part of this building
was badly damaged during
the May blitz and was
demolished. To complete
the picture is a cargo vessel
in the lock with tugs,
bunkering boats, gig boats
and a sailing barge.

The 'Bootle Bull'. c.1906. The Hornby Dock lighthouse was known locally as the 'Bootle Bull', due to the deep resonous bellow of its fog horn. It stood on the north wall of Bootle Docks and was demolished in 1928 to make way for a new lighthouse to be built at Gladstone Dock.

Hornby Dock. c.1909. Bootle dockers are seen unloading beef from the White Star Line ship, *SS Baltic*, at Hornby Dock, Bootle. It was loaded into a refrigeration van that belonged to Aldersons' Depository, Church Street, Bootle. The team of horses belongs to Thomas Wilson, Berry Street, Bootle. This rare photograph was taken by Wright & Co (Bootle).

Gladstone Docks. c.1920. This aerial view shows Bootle's dock system. The second phase of Gladstone Dock is under construction. The first phase was opened by King George V and Queen Mary in 1913. Looking south is Hornby and the Alexandra, Langton, Brocklebank and Canada docks can be seen. The overhead railway to the left winds its way parallel with the inside of the docks until it reaches Strand Road, Bootle where it bends and continues outside the dock wall. Also in view are the Leeds and Liverpool Canal and the Liverpool Southport Railway line.

Opening of Gladstone Dock. c.1927. The second and final phase of Gladstone Dock system, was opened by their Majesties King George V and Queen Mary, just as they opened the first phase in 1913. They sailed from Liverpool Landing Stage, in the Mersey Docks and Harbour Boards own tender, the *Galatea*. They were greeted at the docks by thousands of people, mainly schoolchildren who had been given the day off school. Some of them can be seen lining the dockside. I wonder how many fell into the water that day? As the *Galatea* sailed through the mouth of the dock it broke a tape which had been stretched across the entrance.

Gladstone Dock. c.1966. Berthing three abreast was a rare sight in the docks. This photograph was taken during the 1966 seamen's strike, which lasted for seven weeks. On the left are Canadian Pacific liners, including the *Empress of Canada*. An earlier ship of the same name caught fire and capsized in Gladstone Dock on 25th January 1953. On the right are at least five ships of the Blue Funnel Line, including *Astyanax* and the *Antilochus* - the former being assisted by two tugs of the Rea Towing Co. Ltd.

GLADSTONE DOCKS, BOOTLE.

Gladstone Dock. c.1914. The world's largest ship, the *Aquitania*, edges her way carefully into Gladstone Dock. This beautiful ship must have been a very impressive sight to the dock workers waiting for her to berth. She had arrived in Liverpool to be converted to oil-burning and for the fitting of a gyro-compass.

SS Ivernia. **c.1903.** Sister ship to the *Saxonia* she was built in 1900 by C.S. Swan Hunter, Newcastle. She could accommodate 164 first-class passengers, 200 second-class and 1,600 third-class. Her maiden voyage was from Liverpool to New York on 14th April 1900. Her normal service was Liverpool - Queenstown (Cobh, now the city of Cork)- Boston. In 1911, she entered the New York - Mediterranean service and in 1912 the Fiume – Messina – Naples – Funchal - New York route. In 1917 she was torpedoed by UB-47, 58 miles of Cape Matapan, Italy, with 2,800 troops on board en-route for Alexandria; 87 troops and 36 crew were lost.

RIVER MERSEY—INWARD BOUND

Inward Bound. c.1920. The artist Sam Brown certainly captures the different moods and shipping in the Mersey. With New Brighton pier in the background, a sailing ship enters the Mersey after a long and usually hazardous voyage. Other sailing ships ply their trade, one of which is being assisted by a tug. A Mersey Ferry, the *Lily*, ploughs its way through these ships on its way to Liverpool from New Brighton

Outward Bound. c.1910. Taken from a ferry boat as dusk falls: another ship is about to leave the River Mersey on a voyage to some far distant land. The name of the ship is unknown. She is following another ship out of the river and is just about to pass the Rock Battery and New Brighton Lighthouse.

Towards Evening c.1908.
Evening shadows form on
the Mersey as the day ends,
with the Cunard liner,
Campania, heading off to
New York on another
transatlantic voyage. It is
seen here approaching Perch
Rock Battery and Lighthouse.

Aquitania. **c.1914.** This
four-funnelled Cunard liner
has just left Gladstone lock
and is being assisted by two
of Rea's tugs as she is about
to set sail. Notice New
Brighton Tower in the
background. It stood 621 foot
high, 120 foot taller than
Blackpool Tower. Lack of
maintenance took its toll and
eventually it was dismantled
in 1919. This started the
decline of the resort and the
subsequent closure of the
ferry service in 1971.

Tide Time. p.u.1905. As ships sail out of and into the Mersey, the second resort after New Brighton is Seaforth Sands. This was a very popular day out for all of the family. Apart from having a 'paddle' and enjoying the fresh sea air, one could stand and watch the ships. The photographer had to roll his trousers up to the knees to take this postcard view. In the background is Crosby Road. All this area is now part of the 'Kelloggs' grain storage facility.

SS Snowdon. **p.u.1913.** This is one of the ships that belonged to the Liverpool and North Wales Steamship Company which sailed from Liverpool to the Menai Straits in North Wales. She was built in 1892 at Laird Bros. of Birkenhead with a length of 175 feet and a gross tonnage of 338. She saw many years service before being sold and broken up at Port Glasgow in 1931.

SS La Marguerite. c.1904.
Seen heading up the Menai
Straits on 12th May 1904
after sailing from Liverpool
to Llandudno and the Menai
Straits, prior to regular
sailings later in the month.
The paddle boxes are painted
black, the colour of her
previous owners, but these
were later repainted white to
conform with the rest of the
Liverpool & North Wales
Steamship Company's fleet.
On 28th September 1925 *La
Marguerite* arrived at Menai
Bridge on her final voyage.
Three weeks later she left the
Mersey for the Thomas Ward
breakers' yard at Briton
Ferry.

**The wind-tossed Mersey.
p.u.1911.** Another ship sails
out of the Mersey in a heavy
sea. The postcard was
published by Wright & Co
(Bootle) and the
photographer himself,
William Thomas Wright,
sent this postcard to a friend
saying "I hope you liked the
last postcard I sent. This one
will fit in nicely. I have been
working hard all night in the
darkroom" (developing this
photograph?).

Index

Also of interest:

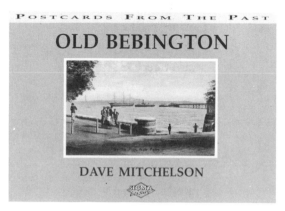

POSTCARDS FROM THE PAST: OLD BEBINGTON

Dave Mitchelson

A nostalgic tour of Bebington, New Ferry, Higher Bebington and surrounding villages illustrated by old and rare picture postcards. Street scenes, notable buildings, local events and transport are all featured. £6.95

POSTCARDS FROM THE PAST: ROCK FERRY

Dave Mitchelson

This is the second book based on the author's extensive collection. Memories will flood back for local people as they see how Rock Ferry was once a leafy village with fine old buildings and fascinating local personalities.
£6.95

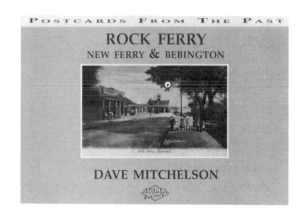

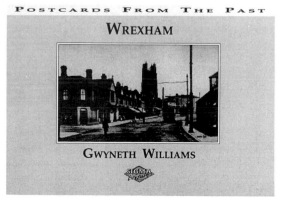

POSTCARDS FROM THE PAST: WREXHAM

Gwyneth Williams

Take a lingering look into Wrexham's past with this excellent selection of black and white postcards. The collection gives an insight into the way that the town has developed over the years, whilst evoking nostalgic memories of the old ways of life. Will fascinate residents and those interested in local history.
£6.95

LIVERPOOL FIRSTS:
Great Merseyside Geniuses

Jack Cooper

Merseysiders are justifiably proud of their reputation as innovators, but sometimes they make claims that cannot be supported - hence this book, which is a serious attempt to produce an accurate account that will be both informative and entertaining. Find out who was first – and with what – and how the world followed in Liverpool's footsteps!
"A marvellous collection to dip into or study cover to cover ... the eminently readable style exemplifies the renowned Merseyside humour." EVENT 15
£6.95

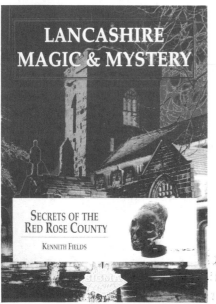

LANCASHIRE MAGIC & MYSTERY:
Secrets of the Red Rose County

Kenneth Fields

Covering all of Lancashire, including Merseyside and Greater Manchester, Ken Field's new book will guide you to places of mystery and curiosity. With tales of hauntings, witchcraft, religious relics, folklore and UFOs, this book is a must for anyone interested in the supernatural. Will appeal to visitors and residents, but also the increasing number of armchair travellers who relish the secret history of the landscape. The author enjoys exploring all aspects of the English countryside and contributes regularly to magazines. This is his fourth book for Sigma.
'It's a smashing read!' ALAN BESWICK- GREATER MANCHESTER RADIO
£6.95